Paranormal Field Guides

HOW TO FIND DRAGONS

Thomas Kingsley Troupe

BLACK
RABBIT
BOOKS

Hi Jinx is published by Black Rabbit Books
P.O. Box 227, Mankato, Minnesota, 56002.
www.blackrabbitbooks.com
Copyright © 2023 Black Rabbit Books

Marysa Storm, editor; Michael Sellner, designer
and photo researcher

Library of Congress Cataloging-in-Publication Data
Names: Troupe, Thomas Kingsley, author.
Title: How to find dragons / Thomas Kingsley Troupe.
Description: Mankato, Minnesota: Black Rabbit Books, 2023. |
Series: Hi jinx. Paranormal field guides | Includes bibliographical references
and index. | Audience: Ages 8-12 | Audience: Grades 4-6 |
Summary: "With fun facts, a colorful design, and critical thinking questions,
How to Find Dragons inspires readers to take their love of the paranormal to
the next level all while laughing and learning"- Provided by publisher.
Identifiers: LCCN 2020034545 (print) | LCCN 2020034546 (ebook) |
ISBN 9781623107178 (hardcover) | ISBN 9781644665664 (paperback) |
ISBN 9781623107239 (ebook)
Subjects: LCSH: Dragons–Juvenile literature.
Classification: LCC GR830.D7 T759 2022 (print) | LCC GR830.D7 (ebook) |
DDC 398.24/54–dc23
LC record available at https://lccn.loc.gov/2020034545
LC ebook record available at https://lccn.loc.gov/2020034546

Image Credits

Shutterstock: Aleksandr Bryliaev, 4; Aluna1,
18; Arcady, 12; Beatriz Gascon J, 14; brux,
17; Christos Georghiou, Cover, 8–9, 13, 15;
DenisKrivoy, 8–9; Dualororua, 10–11; Galyna
G, 3, 4, 7, 8, 9, 13, 16, 17, 18; grafikwork, 1,
21; GraphicsRF.com, 6, 9; HitToon, Cover,
1; jamesjoong, 5; jeffhobrath, 2, 3, 21;
Memo Angeles, Cover, 5, 6, 12–13, 13, 16,
18; monbibi, 4, 5, 9, 14; mspoint, Cover, 1,
21; MSSA, 18; My Life Graphic, 5, 16–17;
Nearbirds, 16–17; Pasko Maksim, 9, 19, 23, 24;
Paulo Resende, 2, 3; Pitju, 7, 11, 17, 21; Ron
Dale, 3, 4, 8, 15, 20; Solomandra, 14; totallypic,
5; Valentyna Chukhlyebova, 10, 20; ViMin, 4, 5,
16, 22, 23; Yevheniia Rodina, 6

CONTENTS

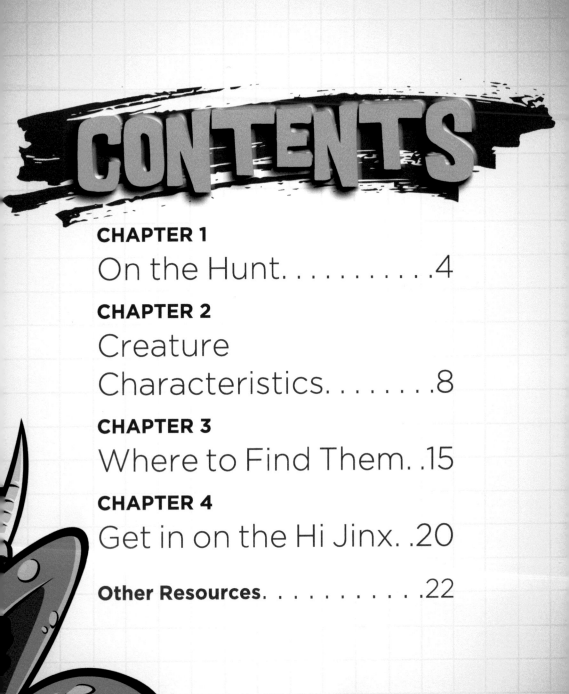

CHAPTER 1
On the Hunt. 4

CHAPTER 2
Creature
Characteristics. 8

CHAPTER 3
Where to Find Them. .15

CHAPTER 4
Get in on the Hi Jinx. .20

Other Resources. 22

ON THE HUNT

I heard you're hoping to find some dragons. Is that right? Well, you've cracked open the right book. I'm a dragon expert. I've survived two dragon attacks. I even flew one across the Pacific Ocean.* This amazing field guide you're holding will help YOU find dragons too!

*Expert's Note

It's OK if you're super impressed. Most people are.

Thomas Kingsley Troupe

Thomas Kingsley Troupe is not well-known for his dragon research. But he sure loves talking about the creatures. Just check out all his claims on the previous page. We asked him if he had any pictures. He said his dog ate them.

Handy and Helpful

You've probably never hunted a monster. That's where my handy guide comes in. This book is all about dragons. You'll soon know what these **reptiles** look like. You'll know what they eat. And yes, you'll know where to find them.

So pack this book with you on your quest! It'll be like I'm right there with you, every step of the way.

Chapter 2

CREATURE CHARACTERISTICS

Before you search for dragons, you must know what they look like. An adult dragon is usually huge. Most are about as big as a garage. Thick, strong scales cover their bodies like armor. They have big, batlike wings and long tails. And their breath? It smells like campfires and dead rats. Most dragons breathe fire. So please don't try to have a burping contest with one.* One fiery belch could set an entire village on fire.

Not all stories say dragons breathe fire. Some say dragons can shoot ice or acid from their mouths.

*Expert's Note

My friend tried having a burping contest with a dragon once. It did not end well.

Behaviors

Dragons are powerful. Their tails can crumble castles and clear entire forests. A dragon can easily knock this book from your hand, so hold it tight! Dragons can also fly. Be careful about that too.

Not all dragons are mean, though. Some are kind, wise, and can even talk. Get them started with a story. They'll never be quiet!

Diet

Most dragons eat farm animals. So leave your pet pig at home when you go hunting. Not all the dragons I've seen eat just meat, though. I've tried to **lure** dragons with different foods. They really seem to love little **appetizer** sandwiches. Some of them can't **resist** snickerdoodle cookies.* Try different foods to see what works best.

*Expert's Note
Sugar cookies work well too.

Some people think the Loch Ness monster might be a dragon.

Chapter 3

WHERE TO FIND THEM

Dragons live all around the world. Most live in mountains. I've found a few in caves. There, they guard huge piles of treasure. Some sneaky dragons like to hide where you'd least expect them, though. For example, I found about 20 dragons at a bowling alley in Ronkonkoma, New York. They were having a **tournament** and eating Hawaiian pizza.

Tracking the Creatures

I'm sorry to say that tracking a dragon isn't easy. When they do leave their homes, they're often flying. Your best bet is to keep your eyes on the skies.

When they are on the ground, dragons leave big, four-toed tracks. Sometimes you'll find tail trails between the tracks. But not always. They hate dragging their tails through mud.

Now What?

You're close to the end of this book. That means you're pretty much a dragon expert. That's great. But what should you do when you find a dragon? Be careful, that's what! Wear something fireproof. The dragon might decide to burp!

And yes, you're quite welcome for all the amazing advice. Thanks to my guide, you'll be able to find dragons.

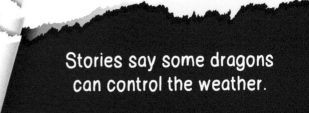

Stories say some dragons can control the weather.

Chapter 4
GET IN ON THE HI JINX

People are pretty sure dragons aren't real. But you can still search for them. Have an adult take you on cave tours. Visit the library and read books about dragons. Search the Internet for articles. But, most importantly, keep your eyes on the skies. Maybe you could prove these great beasts live among us!

Take It One Step More

1. Dragons are known for breathing fire. If you were a dragon, what sort of powerful "breath" would you want? Why?

2. Imagine you found a baby dragon. Would you keep it as a pet? Why or why not?

3. Why do you think people started telling stories about dragons? Research to find out.

GLOSSARY

acid (AHS-id)—a chemical substance that can dissolve things

appetizer (AP-i-tahy-zer)—a small dish of food served before the main part of a meal

claim (KLAYM)—to say something is true when some people might say it's not true

lure (LUHR)—to attract someone or something to an area

reptile (REP-tile)—a cold-blooded animal that breathes air and has a backbone; most reptiles lay eggs and have scaly skin.

resist (ree-ZIST)—to fight against something or try to stop it

tournament (TOOR-nuh-muhnt)—a series of contests played for a championship

BOOKS

Braun, Eric. *Taking Care of Your Dragon.* Caring for Your Magical Pets. Mankato, MN: Black Rabbit Books, 2020.

Gish, Ashley. *Dragons.* Amazing Mysteries. Mankato, MN: Creative Education, 2020.

Owings, Lisa. *Dragons.* Mythical Creatures. Minneapolis: Bellwether Media, Inc., 2021.

WEBSITES

Dragon Facts for Kids
kids.kiddle.co/Dragon

How to Spot a Dragon: Five Dragons from around the World
www.dkfindout.com/us/explore/how-to-spot-dragon-five-dragons-from-around-world/

Totally Crazy Monster Myths (That Are Actually True!)
kids.nationalgeographic.com/explore/monster-myths/

INDEX

B

behaviors, 11, 12, 15,
 16, 17

E

eating, 12, 15

F

features, 8, 9, 11, 17

H

habitats, 15, 20

S

sizes, 8

T

tracking, 16–17